SEALS!

Written by Ellen Catala
Illustrated by Greg Harris

Reviewed by Dr. Edward M. Spevak,
Assistant Curator of Mammals at the Bronx Zoo.

© 2000 McClanahan Book Company, Inc.
All rights reserved.
Published by McClanahan Book Company, Inc.
23 West 26th Street, New York, NY 10010
ISBN: 0-7681-0212-X
Printed in the U.S.A.

They live both in the sea and on land. Some of them weigh as much as rhinoceroses.

SEALS!

ARE SEALS FISH?

No. They are a kind of ocean mammal that scientists call a **pinniped**–which means "fin foot." Like all mammals, including people, seal babies drink milk from their mothers. There are three main kinds of seal.

1. Fur seals and sea lions have ears you can see. They are called **eared seals**.

California Sea Lion

Stellar Sea Lion

Northern Fur Seal

New Zealand Fur Seal

2. **Earless seals**, such as harbor seals, bearded seals, and ringed seals, have ears that don't show on the outside.

Harbor Seal

Kinds of

- eared seals
- earless seals
- walruses

Bearded Seal

3. **Walruses** have tusks!

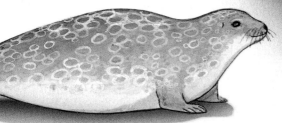

Ringed Seal

Seals range in size from the 4 ton (3,600 kg) southern elephant seal to the 150 pound (68 kg) Baikal seal.

DO SEALS WALK OR SWIM?

Both! But they swim much more gracefully than they walk. Their soft, smooth bodies glide through water. Eared seals swim by moving their powerful front flippers. Earless seals and walruses swim by flapping their wide back flippers.

Water Speeds

- Slowest–walruses travel up to 6 miles per hour (10 kmph)
- Fastest–fur seals and seal lions travel up to 34 mph (55 kmph)

California Sea Lion

Harbor Seal

On land, they move much more slowly. Fur seals, sea lions, and walruses can pull their back flippers under their bodies to use as legs—so they can walk. Earless seals, however, can't use their rear flippers for walking—so they use their front flippers to drag their bodies.

HOW DO SEALS STAY WARM?

They have a thick layer of fat under their skin called **blubber**. The fat keeps their insides warm. And they don't seem to mind cold on their thick skin. Many seals cover themselves with snow and sleep on ice!

A walrus's skin is 2 inches (5 cm) thick!

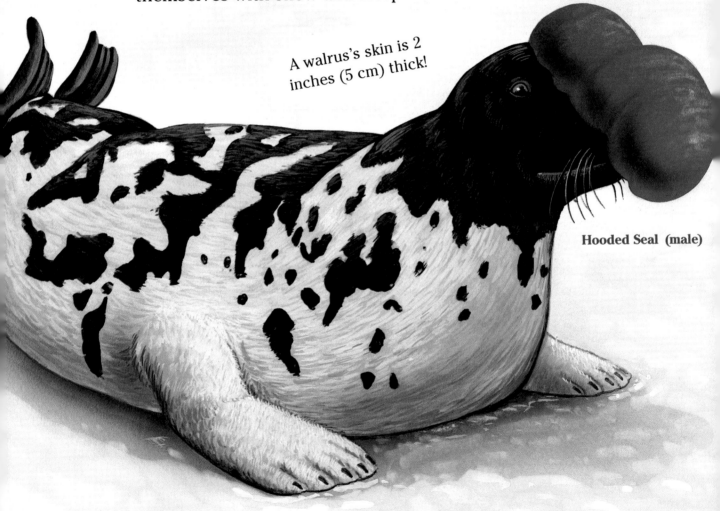

Hooded Seal (male)

Fur seals have a layer of blubber *and* two fur coats to keep them warm. The bottom coat is soft and thick so it traps body heat. While the top coat is coarse and oily so it keeps out water.

Bearded Seal

All seals **molt**—which means they shed their old coats each year to reveal new ones underneath.

CAN SEALS SEE UNDERWATER?

Yes! In fact, seals can see very well in the depths of the ocean where human eyes would see only blackness. Their tear glands put a film of fine clear oil over their eyes. The oil protects against saltwater and blowing snow.

On land, everything they look at is a little blurry. They sometimes mistake a motionless polar bear for a mound of snow. Knowing this, polar bears stand very still if a seal they are stalking looks their way!

WHAT DO SEALS EAT?

Most eat seafood—fish, shellfish, and small ocean animals such as squid. Some seals eat other kinds of animals. The leopard seal eats penguins and seal pups, as well as fish!

Sea lions often swallow rocks. Over 100 were found in the stomach of one animal!

Leopard Seal

Walruses eat huge amounts of food—about 100 pounds (45 kg) a day. They root in the mud at the bottom of the ocean for shellfish. But rogue walruses, which are very rare, eat meat—especially seals!

When fishing is poor, seals can always live off their blubber for a while—but not forever. They need that blubber to stay warm!

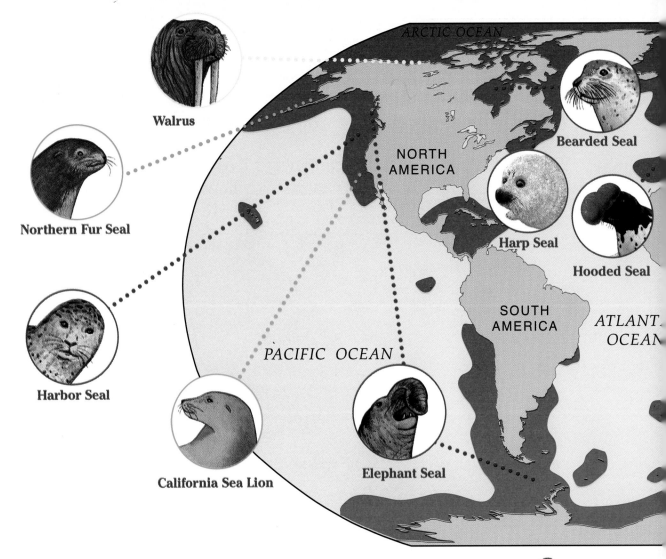

Walrus

Northern Fur Seal

Harbor Seal

California Sea Lion

ARCTIC OCEAN

NORTH AMERICA

Bearded Seal

Harp Seal

Hooded Seal

SOUTH AMERICA

ATLANT. OCEAN

PACIFIC OCEAN

Elephant Seal

WHERE DO SEALS LIVE?

All over the world, but they prefer places that are cold.
Most seals live in salt water. However, the Baikal seal lives
in Lake Baikal in Russia. And a few other kinds of seal also
live in freshwater lakes in very cold regions.

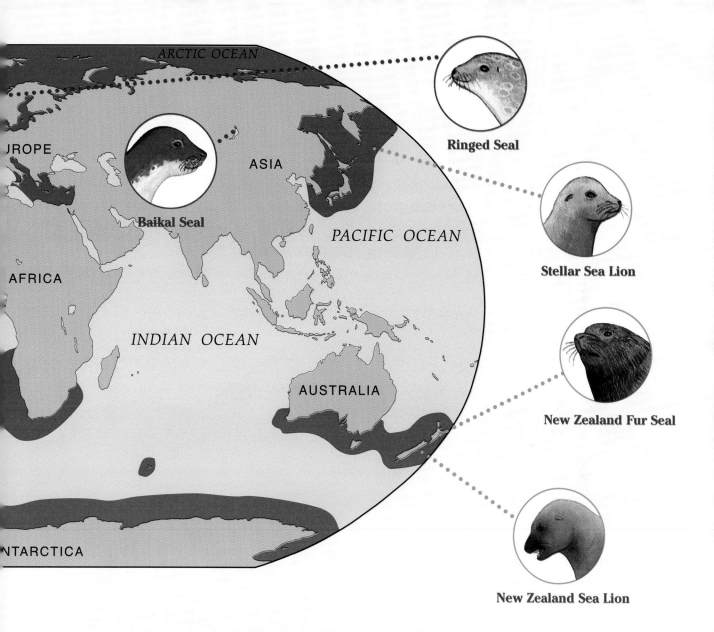

ARCTIC OCEAN

EUROPE

ASIA

AFRICA

PACIFIC OCEAN

INDIAN OCEAN

AUSTRALIA

ANTARCTICA

Baikal Seal

Ringed Seal

Stellar Sea Lion

New Zealand Fur Seal

New Zealand Sea Lion

In general, eared seals meet in big groups, called **rookeries**.
Earless seals are more likely to live alone or in small groups.
But there are exceptions to this rule.

All walruses, except for rogue walruses, live in large groups.

WHAT ABOUT BABIES?

Mother seals give birth to one baby, called a **pup**, about once a year. The mother usually goes to the place where she was born to have her pup.

All seal pups are born either on land or on ice. Harp seals, for example, will only bear their pups on ice.

Great hooded seal pups drink up to 20 pounds (9 kg) of milk every day for four days after they are born!

Hooded Seal

Earless seals that have babies on ice floes do not hunt for food while they are nursing their young. They just live off their fat! These seals do not let their pups out of sight until they are weaned, which is usually 4 days to 8 weeks after birth.

Mother seals recognize their babies by their cry and their smell. The stellar sea lion drops her newborn pup over and over on rocks until it cries, so she can learn to recognize its voice!

New Zealand Sea Lion

Eared seals may nurse their pups from a few months to a year. The mother often leaves her pups from time to time to feed at sea.

Eared seal pups are often in danger of being trampled by adult males, called **bulls**. Some bulls, which may be five times larger than the females, will actually attack and kill pups that get in their way!

Walruses are very good mothers. They keep a close eye on their babies, called **calves**, for two years!

DO SEALS HAVE ANY ENEMIES?

Yes—polar bears, sharks, killer whales, and people. That is why some seals have pups on ice floes—which are hard for their enemies to reach! Walruses are so huge that they have no enemies except for people.

Human hunters in the 18th and 19th Centuries killed so many seals that many species almost became extinct! If only those hunters had followed the wisdom of the Inuit, the native people of the Arctic. The Inuit valued seals because they depended upon them for food, clothes, and some housing materials. They never killed more animals than they needed to survive!

Today, many countries have laws that protect seals.

BET YOU DIDN'T KNOW...

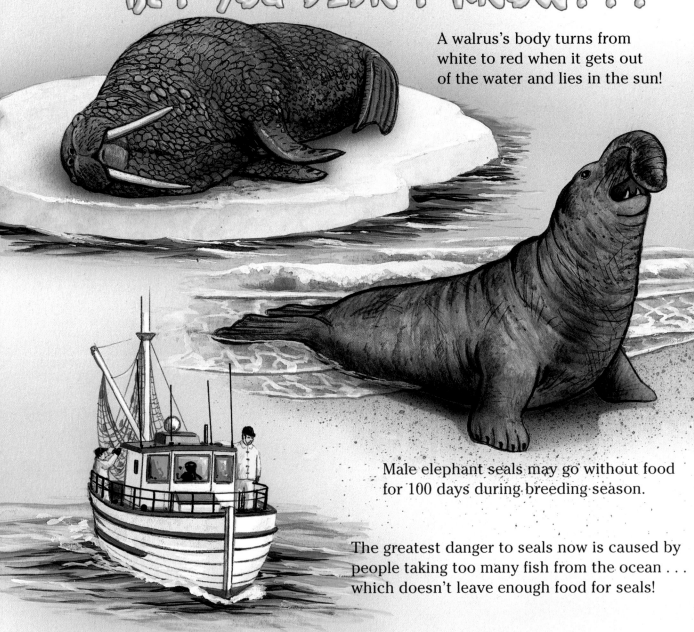

A walrus's body turns from white to red when it gets out of the water and lies in the sun!

Male elephant seals may go without food for 100 days during breeding season.

The greatest danger to seals now is caused by people taking too many fish from the ocean . . . which doesn't leave enough food for seals!

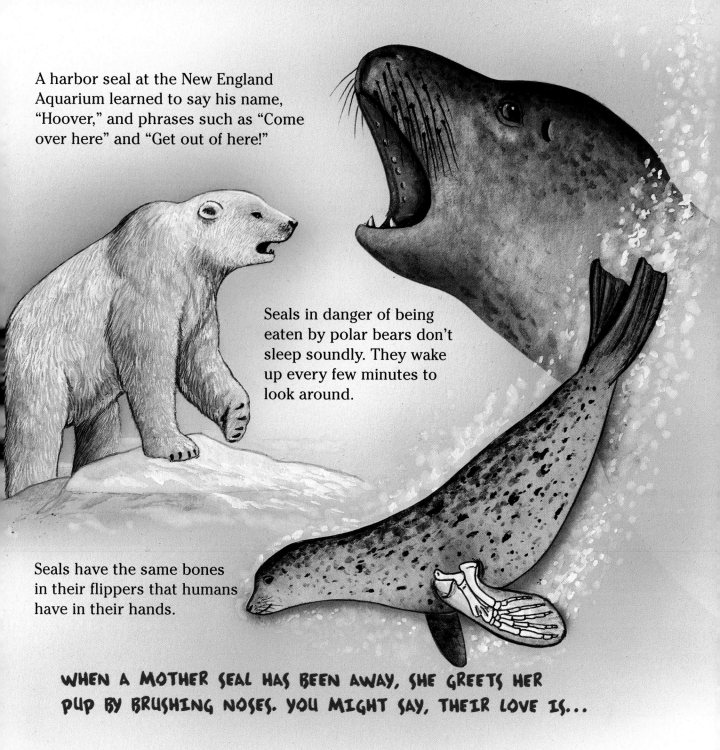

A harbor seal at the New England Aquarium learned to say his name, "Hoover," and phrases such as "Come over here" and "Get out of here!"

Seals in danger of being eaten by polar bears don't sleep soundly. They wake up every few minutes to look around.

Seals have the same bones in their flippers that humans have in their hands.

WHEN A MOTHER SEAL HAS BEEN AWAY, SHE GREETS HER PUP BY BRUSHING NOSES. YOU MIGHT SAY, THEIR LOVE IS...

SEALED WITH A KISS!

Harp Seal